The Burning Wheel

The Burning Wheel
Aldous Huxley

MINT EDITIONS

The Burning Wheel was first published in 1916.

This edition published by Mint Editions 2021.

ISBN 9781513279589 | E-ISBN 9781513284606

Published by Mint Editions®

minteditionbooks.com

Publishing Director: Jennifer Newens
Design & Production: Rachel Lopez Metzger
Project Manager: Micaela Clark
Typesetting: Westchester Publishing Services

Contents

The Burning Wheel	7
Doors of the Temple	9
Villiers de L'Isle-Adam	10
Darkness	11
Mole	12
The Two Seasons	14
Two Realities	15
Quotidian Vision	16
Vision	17
The Mirror	18
Variations on a Theme of Laforgue	19
Philosophy	20
Philoclea in the Forest	21
Books and Thoughts	23
"Contrary to Nature and Aristotle"	24
Escape	25
The Garden	26
The Canal	27

The Ideal Found Wanting	28
Misplaced Love	29
Sonnet	30
Sentimental Summer	31
The Choice	32
The Higher Sensualism	33
Sonnet	34
Formal Verses	35
Perils of the Small Hours	36
Complaint	37
Return to an Old Home	38
Fragment	39
The Walk	40

The Burning Wheel

Wearied of its own turning,
Distressed with its own busy restlessness,
Yearning to draw the circumferent pain—
The rim that is dizzy with speed—
To the motionless centre, there to rest,
The wheel must strain through agony
On agony contracting, returning
Into the core of steel.
And at last the wheel has rest, is still,
Shrunk to an adamant core:
Fulfilling its will in fixity.
But the yearning atoms, as they grind
Closer and closer, more and more
Fiercely together, beget
A flaming fire upward leaping,
Billowing out in a burning,
Passionate, fierce desire to find
The infinite calm of the mother's breast.
And there the flame is a Christ-child sleeping,
Bright, tenderly radiant;
All bitterness lost in the infinite
Peace of the mother's bosom.
But death comes creeping in a tide
Of slow oblivion, till the flame in fear
Wakes from the sleep of its quiet brightness
And burns with a darkening passion and pain,
Lest, all forgetting in quiet, it perish.
And as it burns and anguishes it quickens,
Begetting once again the wheel that yearns—
Sick with its speed—for the terrible stillness
Of the adamant core and the steel-hard chain.
And so once more
Shall the wheel revolve till its anguish cease
In the iron anguish of fixity;
Till once again

Flame billows out to infinity,
Sinking to a sleep of brightness
In that vast oblivious peace.

Doors of the Temple

Many are the doors of the spirit that lead
    Into the inmost shrine:
And I count the gates of the temple divine,
    Since the god of the place is God indeed.
    And these are the gates that God decreed
Should lead to his house:—kisses and wine,
Cool depths of thought, youth without rest,
    And calm old age, prayer and desire,
The lover's and mother's breast,
    The fire of sense and the poet's fire.

But he that worships the gates alone,
    Forgetting the shrine beyond, shall see
    The great valves open suddenly,
Revealing, not God's radiant throne,
    But the fires of wrath and agony.

Villiers de L'Isle-Adam

Up from the darkness on the laughing stage
A sudden trap-door shot you unawares,
Incarnate Tragedy, with your strange airs
Of courteous sadness. Nothing could assuage
The secular grief that was your heritage,
Passed down the long line to the last that bears
The name, a gift of yearnings and despairs
Too greatly noble for this iron age.

Time moved for you not in quotidian beats,
But in the long slow rhythm the ages keep
In their immortal symphony. You taught
That not in the harsh turmoil of the streets
Does life consist; you bade the soul drink deep
Of infinite things, saying: "The rest is naught."

Darkness

My close-walled soul has never known
That innermost darkness, dazzling sight,
Like the blind point, whence the visions spring
In the core of the gazer's chrysolite. . .
The mystic darkness that laps God's throne
In a splendour beyond imagining,
    So passing bright.

But the many twisted darknesses
That range the city to and fro,
In aimless subtlety pass and part
And ebb and glutinously flow;
Darkness of lust and avarice,
Of the crippled body and the crooked heart. . .
    These darknesses I know.

Mole

Tunnelled in solid blackness creeps
The old mole-soul, and wakes or sleeps,
He knows not which, but tunnels on
Through ages of oblivion;
Until at last the long constraint
Of each-hand wall is lost, and faint
Comes daylight creeping from afar,
And mole-work grows crepuscular.
Tunnel meets air and bursts; mole sees
Men hugely walking. . . or are they trees?
And far horizons smoking blue,
And chasing clouds for ever new?
Green hills, like lighted lamps aglow
Or quenching 'neath the cloud-shadow;
Quenching and blazing turn by turn,
Spring's great green signals fitfully burn.
Mole travels on, but finds the steering
A harder task of pioneering
Than when he thridded through the strait
Blind catacombs that ancient fate
Had carved for him. Stupid and dumb
And blind and touchless he had come
A way without a turn; but here,
Under the sky, the passenger
Chooses his own best way; and mole
Distracted wanders, yet his hole
Regrets not much wherein he crept,
But runs, a joyous nympholept,
This way and that, by all made mad—
River nymph and oread,
Ocean's daughters and Lorelei,
Combing the silken mystery,
The glaucous gold of her rivery tresses—
Each haunts the traveller, each possesses
The drunken wavering soul awhile;

Then with a phantom's cock-crow smile
Mocks craving with sheer vanishment.

Mole-eyes grow hawk's: knowledge is lent
In grudging driblets that pay high
Unconscionable usury
To unrelenting life. Mole learns
To travel more secure; the turns
Of his long way less puzzling seem,
And all those magic forms that gleam
In airy invitation cheat
Less often than they did of old.

The earth slopes upward, fold by fold
Of quiet hills that meet the gold
Serenity of western skies.
Over the world's edge with clear eyes
Our mole transcendent sees his way
Tunnelled in light: he must obey
Necessity again and thrid
Close catacombs as erst he did,
Fate's tunnellings, himself must bore
Through the sunset's inmost core.
The guiding walls to each-hand shine
Luminous and crystalline;
And mole shall tunnel on and on,
Till night let fall oblivion.

The Two Seasons

Summer, on himself intent,
    Passed without, for nothing caring
        Save his own high festival.
    My windows, blind and winkless staring,
Wondered what the pageant meant,
        Nor ever understood at all.
And oh, the pains of sentiment!
    The loneliness beyond all bearing. . .
        Mucus and spleen and gall!

But now that grey November peers
    In at my fire-bright window pane?
        And all its misty spires and trees
    Loom in upon me through the rain
And question of the light that cheers
        The room within—now my soul sees
Life, where of old were sepulchres;
        And in these new-found sympathies
Sinks petty hopes and loves and fears,
    And knows that life is not in vain.

Two Realities

A waggon passed with scarlet wheels
    And a yellow body, shining new.
"Splendid!" said I. "How fine it feels
To be alive, when beauty peels
    The grimy husk from life." And you

Said, "Splendid!" and I thought you'd seen
    That waggon blazing down the street;
But I looked and saw that your gaze had been
On a child that was kicking an obscene
    Brown ordure with his feet.

Our souls are elephants, thought I,
    Remote behind a prisoning grill,
With trunks thrust out to peer and pry
And pounce upon reality;
    And each at his own sweet will

Seizes the bun that he likes best
And passes over all the rest.

Quotidian Vision

There is a sadness in the street,
And sullenly the folk I meet
Droop their heads as they walk along,
Without a smile, without a song.
A mist of cold and muffling grey
Falls, fold by fold, on another day
That dies unwept. But suddenly,
Under a tunnelled arch I see
On flank and haunch the chestnut gleam
Of horses in a lamplit steam;
And the dead world moves for me once more
With beauty for its living core.

Vision

I had been sitting alone with books,
    Till doubt was a black disease,
When I heard the cheerful shout of rooks
    In the bare, prophetic trees.

Bare trees, prophetic of new birth,
    You lift your branches clean and free
To be a beacon to the earth,
    A flame of wrath for all to see.

And the rooks in the branches laugh and shout
    To those that can hear and understand;
"Walk through the gloomy ways of doubt
    With the torch of vision in your hand."

The Mirror

Slow-moving moonlight once did pass
Across the dreaming looking-glass,
Where, sunk inviolably deep,
Old secrets unforgotten sleep
Of beauties unforgettable.

But dusty cobwebs are woven now
Across that mirror, which of old
Saw fingers drawing back the gold
From an untroubled brow;
And the depths are blinded to the moon,
And their secrets forgotten, for ever untold.

Variations on a Theme of Laforgue

Youth as it opens out discloses
The sinister metempsychosis
Of lilies dead and turned to roses
Red as an angry dawn.
But lilies, remember, are grave-side flowers,
    While slow bright rose-leaves sail
Adrift on the music of happiest hours;
    And those lilies, cold and pale,
Hide fiery roses beneath the lawn
    Of the young bride's parting veil.

Philosophy

"God needs no christening,"
    Pantheist mutters,
     "Love opens shutters
On heaven's glistening.
Flesh, key-hole listening,
    Hears what God utters" . . .
    Yes, but God stutters.

Philoclea in the Forest

I

'T Was I that leaned to Amoret
With: "What if the briars have tangled Time,
Till, lost in the wood-ways, he quite forget
How plaintive in cities at midnight sounds the chime
Of bells slow-dying from discord to the hush whence
they rose and met.

"And in the forest we shall live free,
Free from the bondage that Time has made
To hedge our soul from its liberty?
We shall not fear what is mighty, and unafraid
Shall look wide-eyed at beauty, nor shrink from its majesty."

But Amoret answered me again:
"We are lost in the forest, you and I;
Lost, lost, not free, though no bonds restrain;
For no spire rises for comfort, no landmark in the sky,
And the long glades as they curve from sight are dark
with a nameless pain.

And Time creates what he devours,—
Music that sweetly dreams itself away,
Frail-swung leaves of autumn and the scent of flowers,
And the beauty of that poised moment, when the day
Hangs 'twixt the quiet of darkness and the mirth of the
sunlit hours."

II

Mottled and grey and brown they pass,
The wood-moths, wheeling, fluttering;
And we chase and they vanish; and in the grass
Are starry flowers, and the birds sing
Faint broken songs of the dying spring.

    And on the beech-bole, smooth and grey,
        Some lover of an older day
Has carved in time-blurred lettering
One word only—"Alas."

III

Lutes, I forbid you! You must never play,
    When shimmeringly, glimpse by glimpse
Seen through the leaves, the silken figures sway
In measured dance. Never at shut of day,
When Time perversely loitering limps
        Through endless twilights, should your strings
        Whisper of light remembered things
    That happened long ago and far away:
Lutes, I forbid you! You must never play. . .

And you, pale marble statues, far descried
    Where vistas open suddenly,
I bid you shew yourselves no more, but hide
Your loveliness, lest too much glorified
        By western radiance slantingly
        Shot down the glade, you turn from stone
        To living gods, immortal grown,
And, ageless, mock my beauty's fleeting pride,
You pale, relentless statues, far descried. . .

Books and Thoughts

Old ghosts that death forgot to ferry
Across the Lethe of the years—
These are my friends, and at their tears
I weep and with their mirth am merry.
On a high tower, whose battlements
Give me all heaven at a glance,
I lie long summer nights in trance,
Drowsed by the murmurs and the scents
That rise from earth, while the sky above me
Merges its peace with my soul's peace,
Deep meeting deep. No stir can move me,
Nought break the quiet of my release:
    In vain the windy sunlight raves
    At the hush and gloom of polar caves.

"Contrary to Nature and Aristotle"

One head of my soul's amphisbaena
Turns to the daytime's dust and sweat;
But evenings come, when I would forget
The sordid strife of the arena.

And then my other self will creep
Along the scented twilight lanes
To where a little house contains
A hoard of books, a gift of sleep.

Its windows throw a friendly light
Between the narrowing shutter slats,
And, golden as the eyes of cats,
Shine me a welcome through the night.

Escape

I seek the quietude of stones
Or of great oxen, dewlap-deep
In meadows of lush grass, where sleep
Drifts, tufted, on the air or drones
On flowery traffic. Sleep atones
For sin, comforting eyes that weep.
O'er me, Lethean darkness, creep
Unfelt as tides through dead men's bones!

In that metallic sea of hair,
Fragrance! I come to drown despair
Of wings in dark forgetfulness.
No love... Love is self-known, aspires
To heights unearthly. I ask less,—
Sleep born of satisfied desires.

The Garden

There shall be dark trees round me:—I insist
On cypresses: I'm terribly romantic—
And glimpsed between shall move the whole Atlantic,
Now leaden dull, now subtle with grey mist,
Now many jewelled, when the waves are kissed
By revelling sunlight and the corybantic
South-Western wind: so, troubled, passion-frantic,
The poet's mind boils gold and amethyst.

There shall be seen the infinite endeavour
Of a sad fountain, white against the sky
And poised as it strains up, but doomed to break
In weeping music; ever fair and ever
Young. . . and the bright-eyed wood-gods as they slake
Their thirst in it, are silent, reverently. . .

The Canal

No dip and dart of swallows wakes the black
Slumber of the canal:—a mirror dead
For lack of loveliness remembered
From ancient azures and green trees, for lack
Of some white beauty given and flung back,
Secret, to her that gave: no sun has bled
To wake an echo here of answering red;
The surface stirs to no leaf's wind-blown track.

Between unseeing walls the waters rest,
Lifeless and hushed, till suddenly a swan
Glides from some broader river blue as day,
And with the mirrored magic of his breast
Creates within that barren water-way
New life, new loveliness, and passes on.

The Ideal Found Wanting

I'm sick of clownery and Owlglass tricks;
Damn the whole crowd of you I I hate you all.
The same, night after night, from powdered stall
To sweating gallery, your faces fix
In flux an idiot mean. The Apteryx
You worship is no victory; you call
On old stupidity, God made to crawl
For tempting with world-wisdom's narcotics.

I'll break a window through my prison! See,
The sunset bleeds among the roofs; comes night,
Dark blue and calm as music dying out.
Is it escape? No, the laugh's turned on me!
I kicked at cardboard, gaped at red limelight;
You laughed and cheered my latest knockabout.

Misplaced Love

Red wine that slowly leaned and brimmed the shell
Of pearl, where lips had touched, as light and swift
As naked petals of the rose adrift
Upon the lazy-luted ritournelle
Of summer bee-song: laughing as they fell,
Gold memories: dream incense, childhood's gift,
Blue as the smoke that far horizons lift,
Tenuous as the wings of Ariel:—

These treasured things I laid upon the pyre;
And the flame kindled, and I fanned it high,
And, strong in hope, could watch the crumbling past.
Eager I knelt before the waning fire,
Phoenix, to greet thine immortality. . .
But there was naught but ashes at the last.

Sonnet

Were I to die, you'd break your heart, you say.
Well, if it do but bend, I'm satisfied—
Bend and rebound—for hearts are temper-tried,
Mild steel, not hardened, with the spring and play
Of excellent tough swords. It's not that way
That you'll be perishing. But when I've died,
When snap! my light goes out, what will betide
You, if the heart-breaks give you leave to stay?

What will be left, I wonder, if you lose
All that you gave me? "All? A year or so
Out of a life," you say. But worlds, say I,
Of kisses timeless given in ecstasy
That gave me Real You. I die: you go
With me. What's left? Limbs, clothes, a pair of shoes? . . .

Sentimental Summer

The West has plucked its flowers and has thrown
Them fading on the night. Out of the sky's
Black depths there smiles a greeting from those eyes,
Where all the Real, all I have ever known
Of the divine is held. And not alone
Do I stand here now… a presence seems to rise:
Your voice sounds near across my memories,
And answering fingers brush against my own.

Yes, it is you: for evening holds those strands
Of fire and darkness twined in one to make
Your loveliness a web of magic mesh,
Whose cross-weft harmony of soul and flesh
Shadows a thought or glows, when smiles awake,
Like sunlight passionate on southern lands.

The Choice

Comrade, now that you're merry
And therefore true,
Say—where would you like to die
And have your friend to bury
What once was you?
"On the top of a hill
With a peaceful view
Of country where all is still?" . . .
Great God, not I!
I'd lie in the street
Where two streams meet
And there's noise enough to fill
The outer ear,
While within the brain can beat
Marches of death and life,
Glory and joy and fear,
Peace of the sort that moves
And clash of strife
And routs of armies fleeing.
There would I shake myself clear
Out of the deep-set grooves
Of my sluggish being.

The Higher Sensualism

There's a church by a lake in Italy
Stands white on a hill against the sky?
And a path of immemorial cobbles
Leads up and up, where the pilgrim hobbles
Past a score or so of neat reposories,
Where you stop and breathe and tell your rosaries
To the shrined terra-cotta mannikins,
That expound with the liveliest quirks and grins
Known texts of Scripture. But no long stay
Should the pilgrim make upon his way;
But as means to the end these shrines stand here
To guide to something holier,
The church on the hilltop.

     Your heaven's so,
With a path leading up to it past a row
Of votary Priapulids;
At each you pause and tell your beads
Along the quintuple strings of sense:
Then on, to face Heaven's eminence,
New stimulated, new inspired.

Sonnet

If that a sparkle of true starshine be
That led my way; if some diviner thing
Than common thought urged me to fashioning
Close-woven links of burnished poetry;
Then all the heaven that one time dwelt in me
Has fled, leaving the body triumphing.
Dead flesh it seems, with not a dream to bring
Visions that better warm immediacy.

Why have my visions left me, what could kill
That feeble spark, which yet had life and heat?
Fulfilment shewed a present rich and fair:
I strive to mount, but catch the nearest still:
Souls have been drowned between heart's beat and beat,
And trapped and tangled in a woman's hair.

Formal Verses

I

Mother of all my future memories,
    Mistress of my new life, which but to-day
Began, when I beheld, deep in your eyes,
My own love mirrored and the warm surprise
    Of the first kiss swept both our souls away,

Your love has freed me; for I was oppressed
    By my own devil, whose unwholesome breath
Tarnished my youth, leaving to me at best
Age lacking comfort of a soul at rest
    And weariness beyond the hope of death.

II

Ah, those were days of silent happiness!
    I never spoke, and had no need to speak,
    While on the windy down-land, cheek by cheek,
The slow-driven sun beheld us. Each caress
Had oratory for its own defence;
And when I kissed or felt her fingers press,
    I envied not Demosthenes his Greek,
Nor Tully for his Latin eloquence.

Perils of the Small Hours

When life burns low as the fire in the grate
And all the evening's books are read,
I sit alone, save for the dead
And the lovers I have grown to hate.

But all at once the narrow gloom
Of hatred and despair expands
In tenderness: thought stretches hands
To welcome to the midnight room

Another presence:—a memory
Of how last year in the sunlit field,
Laughing, you suddenly revealed
Beauty in immortality.

For so it is; a gesture strips
Life bare of all its make-believe.
All unprepared we may receive
Our casual apocalypse.

Sheer beauty, then you seemed to stir
Unbodied soul; soul sleeps to-night,
And love comes, dimming spirit's sight,
When body plays interpreter.

Complaint

I have tried to remember the familiar places,—
    The pillared gloom of the beechwoods, the towns
by the sea,—
I have tried to people the past with dear known faces,
    But you were haunting me.

Like a remorse, insistent, pitiless,
    You have filled my spirit, you were ever at hand;
You have mocked my gods with your new loveliness:
    Broken the old shrines stand.

Return to an Old Home

In this wood—how the hazels have grown!—
I left a treasure all my own
Of childish kisses and laughter and pain;
Left, till I might come back again
To take from the familiar earth
My hoarded secret and count its worth.
And all the spider-work of the years,
All the time-spun gossamers,
Dewed with each succeeding spring;
And the piled up leaves the Autumns fling
To the sweet corruption of death on death. . .
At the sudden stir of my spirit's breath
All scattered. New and fair and bright
As ever it was, before my sight
The treasure lay, and nothing missed.
So having handled all and kissed,
I put them back, adding one new
And precious memory of you.

Fragment

We're German scholars poring over life,
As over a Greek manuscript that's torn
And stained beyond repair. Our eyes of horn
Read one or two poor letters; and what strife,
What books on books begotten for their sake!
But we enjoy it; and meanwhile neglect
The line that's left us perfect from the wrecked
Rich argosy, clear beyond doubts to make
Conjectures of. So in my universe
Of scribbled half-hid meanings you appear,
Sole perfect symbol of the highest sphere;
And life's great matrix crystal, whose depths nurse
Soul's infinite reflections, glows in you
With now uncertain radiance. . .

The Walk

I. Through the Suburbs

Provincial Sunday broods above the town:
The street's asleep; through a dim window drifts
A small romance that hiccoughs up and down
An air all trills and runs and sudden lifts
To yearning sevenths poised. . . not Chopin quite,
But, oh, romantic; a tinsel world made bright
With rose and honeysuckle's paper blooms,
And where the moon's blue limelight and the glooms
Of last-act scenes of passion are discreet.
And when the tinkling stops and leaves the street
Blank in the sunlight of the afternoon
You feel a curtain dropped. Poor little tune!
Perhaps our grandmother's dull girlhood days
Were fired by you with radiances of pink,
Heavenly, brighter far than she could think
Anything might be. . . till a greater blaze
Tinged life's horizon, when he kissed her first,
Our grandpapa. But a thin ghost still plays
In music down the street, echoing the plaint
Of far romance with its own sadder song
Of Everyday; and as they walk along, . . .
The young man and the woman, deep immersed
In all the suburb-comedy around. . .
They seem to catch coherence in the sound
Of that ghost-music, and the words come faint:—
    Oh the months and the days,
    Oh sleeps and dinners,
    Oh the planning of ways
    And quotidian means!
  Oh endless vistas of mutton and greens,
  Oh weekly mimblings of prayer and praise,
    Oh Evenings with All the Winners!
  Monday sends the clothes to the wash

And Saturday brings them home again:
Mon Dieu, la vie est par trop moche
And Destiny is a sale caboche;
    But I'll give you heaven
    In a dominant seven,
And you shall not have lived in vain.

"In vain," the girl repeats, "in vain, in vain. . ."
Your suburb's whole philosophy leads there.
The ox-stall for our happiness, for pain,
Poignant and sweet, the dull narcotic ache
Of wretchedness, and in resigned despair
A grim contentment. . . ashen fruits to slake
A nameless, quenchless thirst. The tinkling rain
Of that small sentimental music wets
Your parching suburb: it may sprout. . . who knows? . . .
In something red and silken like a rose,
In sheaves of almost genuine violets.

Faint chords, your sadness, secular, immense,
Brims to the bursting this poor Actual heart.
For surging through the floodgates that the sense
On sudden lightly opens sweeps the Whole
Into the narrow compass of its part.

He

Inedited sensation of the soul!
You'd have us bless the Hire-Purchase System,
Which now allows the poorest vampers
To feel, as they abuse their piano's dampers,
That angels have stooped down and kissed 'em
With Ave-Maries from the infinite.
But poor old Infinite's dead. Long live his heir,
Lord Here-and-Now. . . for all the rest
Is windy nothingness, or at the best
Home-made Chimera, bodied with despair,
Headed with formless, foolish hope.

She

                        No, no!
We live in verse, for all things rhyme
With something out of space and time.

He

But in the suburb here life needs must flow
In journalistic prose. . .

She

                     But we have set
Our faces towards the further hills, where yet
The wind untainted and unbound may blow.

               II. From the Crest

So through the squalor, till the sky unfolds
To right and left its fringes, penned no more,
A thin canal, 'twixt shore and ugly shore
Of hovels, poured contiguous from the moulds
Of Gothic horror. Town is left at last,
Save for the tentacles that probe, . . . a squat
Dun house or two, allotments, plot on plot
Of cabbage, jejune, ripe or passed,
Chequering with sick yellow or verdigris
The necropolitan ground; and neat paved ways
That edge the road. . . the town's last nerves. . . and cease,
As if in sudden shame, where hedges raise
Their dusty greenery on either hand.
Their path mounts slowly up the hill;
And, as they walk, to right and left expand
The plain and the golden uplands and the blue
Faint smoke of distances that fade from view;
And at their feet, remote and still?
The city spreads itself.

He

That glabrous dome that lifts itself so grand,
There in the marish, is the omphalos,
The navel, umbo, middle, central boss
Of the unique, sole, true Cloud-Cuckoo Land.
Drowsy with Sunday bells and Sunday beer
Afoam in silver rumkins, there it basks,
Thinking of labours past and future tasks
And pondering on the end, forever near,
Yet ever distant as the rainbow's spring.
For still in Cuckoo-Land they're labouring,
With hopes undamped and undiscouraged hearts:
A little musty, but superb, they sit,
Piecing a god together bit by bit
Out of the chaos of his sundered parts.
Unmoved, nay pitying, they view the grins
And lewd grimaces of the folk that jeer. . .
The vulgar herd, gross monster at the best,
Obscenum Mobile, the uttermost sphere,
Alas, too much the mover of the rest,
Though they turn sungates to its widdershins. . .

And in some half a million years perhaps
God may at last be made. . . a new, true Pan,
An Isis templed in the soul of man,
An Aphrodite with her thousand paps
Streaming eternal wisdom.
Yes, and man's vessel, all pavilioned out
With silk and flags in the fair wind astream,
Shall make the port at last, with a great shout
Ringing from all her decks, and rocking there shall dream
For ever, and dream true. . . calm in those roads
As lovers' souls at evening, when they swim
Between the despairing sunset and the dim
Blue memories of mountains lost to sight
But, like half fancied, half remembered episodes
Of childhood, guessed at through the veils of night.
And the worn sailors at the mast who heard

The first far bells and knew the sound for home,
Who marked the land-weeds and the sand-stained foam
And through the storm-blast saw a wildered bird
Seek refuge at the mast-head. . . these at last
Shall earn due praise when all the hubbub's past;
And Cuckoo-Landers not a few shall prove.

She

You have fast closed the temple gates;
    You stand without in the noon-tides glow,
But the innermost darkness, where God waits,
    You do not know, you cannot know.

A Note About the Author

Aldous Huxley (1894–1963) was an English writer and philosopher. Born in Godalming, Huxley—the grandson of famed zoologist Thomas Henry Huxley and grandnephew of poet and critic Matthew Arnold—was raised in a family with wide-ranging intellectual interests. He attended Eton College as a youth before enrolling at Balliol College, Oxford, where he studied English literature and edited *Oxford Poetry*. An eye disease Huxley contracted around this time ended his hopes of studying medicine and serving in the Great War, and he instead graduated with a BA in 1916. After a brief stint teaching French at Eton College—among his pupils was Eric Blair, later to write under the pen-name George Orwell—and several years working for Brynner and Mond, a chemical company, Orwell began writing in earnest. The first decade of his career saw him publish four novels, including *Crome Yellow* (1921) and *Point Counter Point* (1928). These early works of social satire, inspired in part by his acquaintance with members of the Bloomsbury Group, including Bertrand Russell and Alfred North Whitehead, as well as by his friendship with D.H. Lawrence, gave way in the 1930s to more serious works of fiction, including the dystopian classic *Brave New World* (1932) and *Eyeless in Gaza* (1936), a novel with pacifist themes. In 1937, Huxley moved with his wife, Maria, and son, Matthew, to Los Angeles, where he would live, apart from a period in Taos, New Mexico, for the rest of his life. Over the next three decades, Huxley continued to publish award-winning works of fiction, devoted himself to Vedantism, and wrote works on mysticism, Eastern and Western philosophies, and the use of psychedelic drugs.

A Note from the Publisher

Spanning many genres, from non-fiction essays to literature classics to children's books and lyric poetry, Mint Edition books showcase the master works of our time in a modern new package. The text is freshly typeset, is clean and easy to read, and features a new note about the author in each volume. Many books also include exclusive new introductory material. Every book boasts a striking new cover, which makes it as appropriate for collecting as it is for gift giving. Mint Edition books are only printed when a reader orders them, so natural resources are not wasted. We're proud that our books are never manufactured in exce
quantity they need to be read and enjoyed.

Discover more of your favorite classics with Bookfinity™.

- Track your reading with custom book lists.
- Get great book recommendations for your personalized Reader Type.
- Add reviews for your favorite books.
- AND MUCH MORE!

Visit **bookfinity.com** and take the fun Reader Type quiz to get started.

Enjoy our classic and modern companion pairings!

www.ingramcontent.com/pod-product-compliance
Lightning Source LLC
Chambersburg PA
CBHW032115040426
42337CB00041B/1332